Tableau
Questions & Answers

Guide to Tableau concepts and FAQs

Chandraish Sinha

Copyright © 2016

www.LearnTableauPublic.com

Legal Notes

About The Author

Chandraish Sinha has 18 years of experience in implementing Business Intelligence solutions. His experience involves working in different BI applications. He has worked in multiple Tableau end-to-end implementations.

He coaches organizations and consultants in exploring the visualization world of Tableau.

He has a passion for Tableau and shares his knowledge through his blog (http://www.learntableaupublic.com/).

Other book/s written by the Author - Tableau Dashboards, QlikView Essentials and QlikView Questions & Answers.

Table of Contents

1. Understanding the Basics..8

2. All About Data connections.......................................24

3. Calculations in Tableau...38

4.Visualizations..49

5. Dashboards and Visual Story.....................................63

6.Commonly Asked Questions..69

Preface

Tableau is becoming popular with organizations worldwide. The popularity of Tableau is due to the fact that Tableau can extract huge amounts of data and present it in a format that is easy to understand and interpret.

The Objective of this book is to help in quick understanding of Tableau concepts.

This book explains concepts in a very easy-to-understand Question-and-Answer format. Topics are explained with scenarios.

About this book

Chapter1. Understanding the Basics

This Chapter provides an overview of BI and Tableau concepts.

Chapter2. All about Data Connections

In this chapter, you can learn about creating data connections. This chapter provides details on creating data connections, data sources and data preparation in Tableau.

Chapter3. Calculations in Tableau

Calculations enhance your application and provide users meaningful results. This chapter talks about different calculations available in Tableau – regular calculations, Table calculations and Level of Details (LOD).

Chapter4. Visualizations

This chapter deals with different concepts in creating different types of visualizations such as Bar chart, Trend Chart and Maps.

Chapter5. Dashboard and Visual Story
This chapter provides details on how to create dashboards from Sheets. It also shows how to represent data in visual story.
Chapter6. Commonly Asked Questions
This chapter provides answers to commonly asked questions in Tableau. These questions will be helpful in any technical discussion.

How to use this Book

This book provides all the Tableau concepts in a Question-and-Answer format. The book presents scenarios and explanations. To make best use of the book, try to understand each scenario and explore using Tableau Desktop.
To recreate scenario's presented in this book, download **Tableau desktop**. Tableau desktop can be downloaded for free from http://www.tableau.com/products/desktop
By default it downloads a 64-bit windows version. A 32-bit windows version or mac-version is also available.
Tableau desktop free version is a trial version and is available only for two weeks. College students can get one year of Tableau license. Trial version allows you to use file based data sources such as Ms-excel, Text or Access files. Connection to other data sources are only allowed with the licensed version.

Who needs this book?

This book is for novice Tableau developers who want to speed up their Tableau Learning. This book will work as a hand-book that answers all your questions. It will be a good resource to brush up Tableau concepts.
This book provides quick learning by explaining answers to different scenarios.
This book will prepare developers for any technical discussion on Tableau development.

Data used in the book

This book provides exercises which will help readers in better understanding of the concepts. You can create the exercises by using the sample data source provided by Tableau.

After Tableau desktop installation, locate folder **My Tableau Repository** under "My documents" folder.

Under "My Tableau Repository", look for "**Datasources**" sub-folder. This folder contains Tableau provided data source - **Sample- Superstore.xls**. This datasource can be used to complete the exercises.

Sample Workbook

This book also comes with Tableau Solution workbook - Tableau_QA_SolutionsWorkBook.twbx. To obtain this workbook, after your purchase, send an email titled "Requesting Tableau_QA Solution workbook" to chandraish@gmail.com with your Amazon Order number.

Other Resources

http://www.tableau.com/ is a good resource for information on Tableau. Visit http://www.tableau.com/learn/training for free online videos provided by Tableau.

Also visit Author's blog http://www.learntableaupublic.com/ to continue your learning with advanced Tableau concepts and discussions.

1
Understanding the Basics

Q1. What is Tableau?
Ans.
Tableau is a Business Intelligence Application. Tableau is used to create visualizations and interpret data. Tableau follows the basic principles of BI i.e. extracting raw data, transforming it and presenting the data visually so that Business users can make informed decisions.

Q2. Explain Tableau Architecture?
Ans.
Tableau Architecture follows as below

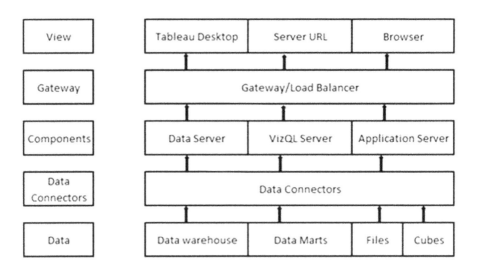

- **Data.** Tableau can connect to any format of source data.
- **Data Connectors.** Tableau provides over 40 optimized data connectors. To various data sources such as MS Excel, MS SQL Server, Google Big Query, Amazon RedShift, Oracle and others.

- It also provides a generic ODBC connector for systems without a native connector.
  Data can be used in-memory or live.
- **Components.** The following components handle the server operations
    - **Application server.** Application Server processes (wgserver.exe) handle content browsing, Server-Administration and authentication to Tableau server web and mobile interfaces.
    - **VizQL Server.** When a user/client requests a visualization, it sends a request to VizQL process (Vizqlserver.exe). The VizQL process in turn sends queries to the data source, returning a result set in the form of images.
    - **Data Server.** It facilitates the management of Data sources on the server.
- **Gateway/Load balancer.** Gateway directs requests to other components.
- **View.** User can view Tableau dashboards thru Tableau desktop or via zero footprint HTML 5 in a web or mobile browser.

Q3. What are the different components of Tableau?
Ans.
Basic components of Tableau are Tableau Desktop, Tableau reader and Tableau Server.
- Developer uses **Tableau desktop** to create visualizations, dashboards and stories.
- Dashboards can be deployed on the **Tableau Server**. Users can access dashboards stored on the server through server URL.
- Tableau desktop can use data as a **"Live"** connection or as an **"Extract"** (TDE).

- Data connection/s used in developing dashboards is reusable. It can be published to the server. Data load schedules can be created to meet the user requirements.
- Tableau desktop design file is called a "Workbook". It has an extension **.twb**.
- Tableau workbooks can also be packaged with data. This packaged workbook is a zip file with extension **.twbx**.
- In the absence of the server, Tableau design files can be viewed by using **Tableau Reader**. Tableau reader is also a free download and can open twbx files.

Q4. Why Tableau is preferred by the business community?
Ans.
- Tableau using the powerful visualization, helps in understanding the data.
- Tableau dashboards are interactive and displays the whole picture of the data. All the data is present, data analysis across different time periods and dimensions is faster.
- Datasource used in the dashboard design can be shared with other developers and users, this helps in maintaining the single version of the truth.
- Development is faster as compared to other applications. Tableau provides easy to use functionalities to create data hierarchy, calculated fields, filters, parameters, Sets and Bins.
- Development is not IT centric. It gives power to the business users. Users can design their own dashboards.
- Creating worksheets, dashboards and stories is easy.
- Based on the data, Tableau's "Show Me" feature suggest user the best visualization type to use. This helps novice users in creating meaningful charts and tables.

- Tableau can handle huge amounts of data. Connection to the data can be live or to an extract.
- For quick review, workbooks can be emailed as packaged workbooks with data.
- Publishing to the server and applying security is easy.

Q5. How Tableau development environment works?
Ans.
Tableau development environment works as follows,

- Tableau desktop is used for creating visualizations such as charts, tables and Maps.
- User can connect to any data source. If multiple tables are used, then these tables can be joined. Data Sources can be named and shared.
- When the data source is created, depending on the data type, Tableau automatically segregates data into measures and dimensions. Data elements can be transformed.
- These data elements are used to create charts, tables and Maps by simple drag-and-drop of data elements into the development area.
- One visualization is created per "worksheet". Multiple worksheets make one "dashboard".
- If the user needs a "story", worksheets and dashboards can be used to create a story.
- Worksheet, Dashboards and Story is created by clicking on the icons at the bottom of the screen

Or by using the menu options

Worksheet	Dashboard	Story

Q6. Explain My Tableau Repository folder?
Ans.
When Tableau desktop is installed, Tableau creates a folder called "My Tableau Repository" in \Documents folder. The folder contains all the files required by Tableau

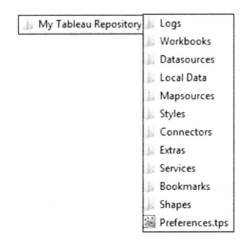

• **Logs**, folder contains all the issue logs.

• **Workbooks**, contains all the workbooks – twb and twbx files. Save all your workbooks in this folder.

• **Datasources**, this folder is used to keep all the datasource files such as csv, excel etc.

• **Local Data**, when custom geocoding is imported, it gets stored in this folder.

• **Mapsources**, Tableau Map Source (.tms) file is stored in this folder.

• **Bookmarks**, with .tbm file extension are stored in this folder.

• **Shapes**, this folder contains all the shapes provided by Tableau. To add your custom shapes, copy custom shapes in an image format and add to a new folder under this folder.

• **Preference.tps**, file is used to add custom color palettes.

Q7. Give an Overview of Tableau Desktop

Ans.

Tableau desktop is a development environment and provides functionality to develop interactive dashboards.

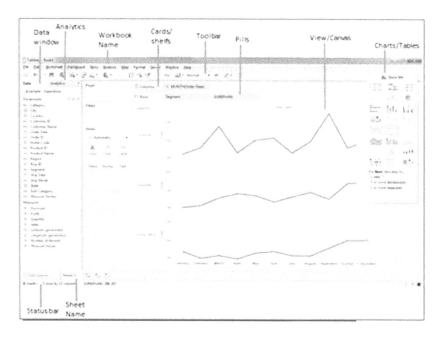

1. **Data window.** Displays information about the data connection and fields in the data source.

2. **Analytics.** Contains ready-to use objects for faster analysis of data.

3. **Workbook Name.** Workbook consists of data connection, work sheet, dashboard, stories and images. Worksheet name has an extension of .twb. If it is a packaged workbook then the extension is .twbx.

4. **Cards/shelves.** Views are created by placing fields on the cards or shelves. **Mark** cards have different shelves such as color, size, label, detail, tooltip. Fields can be placed on these shelves. Changing the Mark type like Automatic, Shape will change these shelves.

5. **Toolbar.** Toolbar provide quick access to different functionalities such as undo/redo, adding sheets, sorting, displaying labels and so on.

6. **Pills.** Fields or calculations on the rows or columns are called Pills. Click on a pill to access pull down menu options such as filter, Table calculations etc. Dimension pill is **blue** in color and Measure pill is **green**.

7. **View/Canvas.** This space displays visualization created by the fields placed on the shelves.

8. **Filters.** Filter shelf is used to place filters that limit the data.

9. **Pages.** This shelf displays views into different pages. If a dimension is placed on Pages, it creates separate pages for each dimension. If a measure is used, then measure is converted to discreet measure.

10. **Show Me.** Depending on the field selection in the data window, Tableau suggests the best suited visualization. Different visualizations can be selected in the "Show Me" box.

11. **Status bar.** Displays various attributes of the visualization in the current worksheet. It displays information such as number of Marks, number of rows and columns and aggregated measure.

12. **Sheet Name.** Displays the name of the current worksheet. Give meaningful names to the sheets, if multiple sheets are created. There are three types of sheets - worksheet, dashboards and story.

Exercise:
Launch Tableau Desktop, connect to datasource **Sample – Superstore.xls** under \Documents\My Tableau Repository\Datasources\. Use **Orders** datasheet as the source data.
Refer to downloaded workbook –
Tableau_QA_SolutionsWorkBook.twbx.

Q8. What are the different responsibilities of a Tableau professional?

Ans.

A Tableau professional's responsibilities may differ based on specific organization but at high-level it consists of

- Understanding the business requirements.
- Analyzing data sources and relationships.
- Extracting data from the required data sources. Making decisions in collaboration with Business users on connecting data live or as an extract.
- Applying required data transformations, creating calculations, Sets, Bins as driven by the requirements.
- Creating visualizations that helps in answering business questions. These visualizations are created and displayed in Sheets, dashboards and stories.
- Deploying the dashboards on the server

Q9. What data sources can be used with Tableau?

Ans.

Tableau can be used with variety of data sources. This includes excel, csv, Multi-dimensional cubes, MS –access and also relational databases, cloud based data sources.

Q10. What is a KPI?

Ans.

Every organization has certain measures that are used to evaluate performance. These measures or indicators are called Key Performance Indicators (KPI). KPI's are different for different organizations, for example, for a Staffing company, one for the KPI may be # of Consultants working at the client site, for a hospital it may be the number for patients treated.

Q11. How is source control performed in Tableau?
Ans.
Tableau can be integrated to source control applications like Microsoft TFS (Team Foundation Server).

Q12. What data sources can be used with Tableau?
Ans.
Tableau can be used with variety of data sources. This includes excel, csv, Multi-dimensional cubes, MS –access and also relational databases, cloud based data sources.

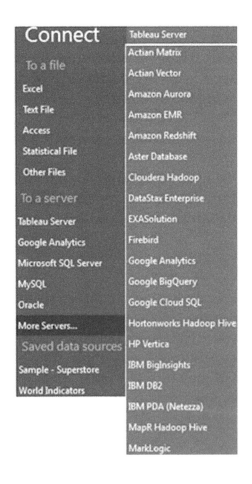

Q13. What is Tableau Development life cycle?
Ans.
Typical Tableau implementation follows these principles,

- Requirement gathering. Discussion with users to understand their data and visualization requirements.
- Analyze data sources. Gather information on different data sources and relationships among the data elements.
- Create mockups of the dashboards. User review of mockups.
- Create data source.
- Structure the data by renaming data fields to user friendly columns. As required, create calculated fields, hierarchies, parameters and other elements.
- Depending on the number of data elements in the datasource, organize data into different folders.
- Create worksheets and dashboards as per the requirement.
- Unit Testing. Comparing the data in the visualizations with the source data.
- Review of dashboard by the users.
- If server option is available and desired deploy dashboards over the Server.
- Create data load schedules.

Q14. What are dimension and fact Tables?
Ans.
Dimension tables, also referred as Dimensions contain the descriptive attribute of the data element. Example of a Dimension table, will be a Customer Dimension, containing fields that describe a customer, i.e. Customer Name, Address and so on. Dimensions are used to slice the data. Primary key in a Dimension table also referred as Dim ID uniquely identifies each row.

Fact table contains measurable attribute of the data. For example, Fact table can contain Sales Amount or the Sales made to a Customer. Fact table contains the foreign key of the Dimension Table.

Dimension provide context to a Fact. Without Dimension Fact will not be meaning full.

In the above example, Customer Info will be stored in Customer Dimension, and Sales made to different customers will be stored in Fact table. These two tables will be **joined** to get Sales Amount of a Customer.

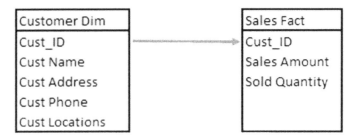

Q15. Given an ER diagram, how you will identify fact and dimension tables

Ans.

- Cardinality between Dimension and Fact is one to many, with many on the Fact side. Look for One to Many relationship in the ER diagram.
- Dimension contains the textual/ descriptive attribute and Fact contains the measureable data. Look for such data elements in the tables.
- Fact table contains the foreign key of the dimension table.

Q16. What is star schema?

Ans.

Star schema is a data structure in which a Fact table is at the center surrounded by dimension tables. The structure looks like a Star and hence the name.

Using below Star schema, you can slice Sales Amount and Quantity by Customer, Time period, Product and Regions.

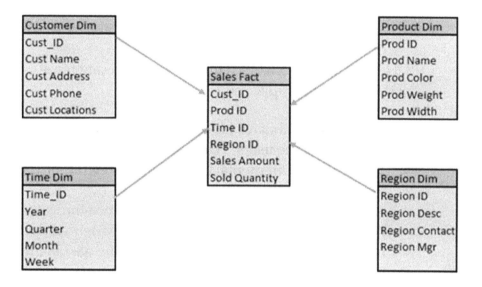

Q17. What is a Snow flake scheme?

Ans. In Star schema, Fact is at the center and surrounded by dimension tables. Snow flake schema is similar to star schema. In Snow flake schema, dimension table/s may be connected to other related dimensions. For example, Product dimension may connect to Category dimension.

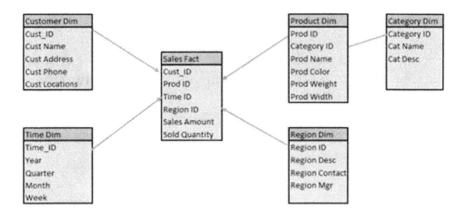

Q18. How will you perform requirement gathering for a Dash boarding application?

Ans.

When creating a dashboard, it is important to get the requirements from the users. When gathering requirements,

- Take data requirements. Data sources, key filters, data refresh frequency.
- Ask users about the KPI (Key performance Indicators).
- Inquire about the questions users are trying to answer.
- Document business rules required for the dashboards.
- Understand security requirements.
- Gather details about any existing reports or desired visualization.
- Provide layout of the screen in terms of dashboard-charts and tables in excel or hand drawn. Get users feedback on the layout.
- Get requirements about the screen resolution.

Q19. What's the difference between a primary key and foreign key in SQL?
Ans.
Primary key uniquely identifies a record in a table. Primary key in one table is referenced by foreign key in another table. Two relational tables are linked based on primary key and foreign key.

Q20. What are some of the joins in SQL?
Ans.
The joins in SQL are
- Inner Join. Returns matching rows from both the tables.
- Left/Outer join. Returns all rows from the left table and the matched rows from the right table
- Right/Outer join. Returns all rows from the Right table and the matched rows from the left table
- Full/Outer join. Returns all rows from table1 and from the table2.It combines the result of both LEFT and RIGHT joins.
- Cartesian join. Join of every row of one table to every row of another table.

Q21. What is the difference between Union and Union All in SQL?
Ans.
Union and Union All are used to combine results of queries. Union eliminates the duplicate records and Union All includes all the records.

Q22. What is data granularity?
Ans.
Data granularity refers to the level of detail or depth of data.

It means the level at which data is stored in a fact table. For e.g. if data is stored at the Year level then it is at the lower granularity. If the data is stored at the Month or day level then it at higher granularity.

Q23. What is meant by data transformation?
Ans.
Data transformation means transforming the data from its original format. Raw data may be in a different format then required by the report or dashboard. Data transformation is required to make the data more suited for the application. An example, can be, removing time information from the DateTime field.

Q24. What is the meaning of discreet and continuous data?
Ans.
Data can be discreet or continuous.
Discreet data contains specific categories. For example, Regions - South and North or Years like 2011, 2012.
Continuous data, on the other hand, is defined by a range and it can take any value over a continuous range.
In Tableau, Dimensions are discreet and Measures are continuous.

Q25. How discreet and continuous data affects the color in visualization?
Ans.
Dimensions are discreet and when dropped on the **Color** shelf displays different colors or color palette.
Measures are continuous and when dropped on the **Color** shelf shows a gradient color.

Q26. How can workbooks be viewed by users in Tableau?
Ans.
Workbooks can be published on Tableau Online or Tableau server.
In the absence of Tableau Server, Workbooks can also be viewed using Tableau Reader. Tableau reader accepts Tableau packaged workbook (twbx) which contain data.

2
All About Data connections

Q27. How to connect to data in Tableau?

Ans.

When Tableau desktop is launched it provides an option to connect to the data. Tableau can connect to a variety of data sources.

- When connecting to data, Tableau provides an option to connect to data Live or as an Extract.
- Data can be extracted to a .tde file. Extracts are faster than live connection.
- When data is extracted, the symbol of the data source changes in the data window. It shows up with two cylinders.

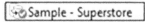

- Data Source can be saved as TDS file or published to Tableau Server.

Exercise:

Use Tableau sample data source **Sample- Superstore.xls** located under \My Tableau Repository\Data sources.

Connect to data live or as an extract.

When connected as an extract, it will provide an option to save the data source as TDE file.

Q28. What are Dimensions and Measures fields in Tableau?

Ans.

When a datasource is created, Tableau automatically segregates data into Dimensions and Measure fields.

- Dimension fields contain the **textual** attribute of the data. It provides the context to the Measure. Dimensions are generally used to create labels and filters. Dimensions are **discreet** and appear **blue** in color in the data pane and the view.
- Measure fields contain the **measureable** attribute of the data - such as Revenue, Profit or Population. Measures are continuous. They are axis in the charts and appear green color. Measures are analyzed by dimensions.

Q29. A query is created and tested in a SQL editor like TOAD or SQL Developer. How can you use this query in Tableau?
Ans.
Tableau provides an option to write custom query in **New Custom SQL**.
A pre-built query can be copied/pasted in the query editor.
The Developer can also use this space to write a custom query.
New Custom SQL option is available when connected to relational data sources.

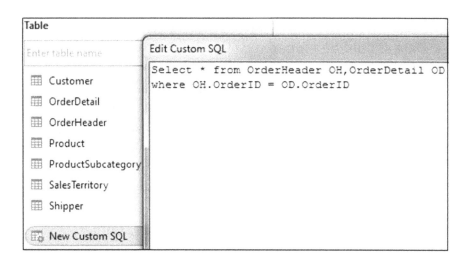

Q30. How is data prepared for analysis?
Ans.
Data source preparation also called as data transformation is an important step in dash boarding. Data Source preparation depends on the Business and visualization requirements.

- Review your source data to see if data is formatted correctly. If multiple tables or excel sheets are involved, look for the relationships between them. Create appropriate joins.
- For successful visualization, data should have dimensions and measures.
- If the source data contains a wrongly formatted Excel file, utilize **Data Interpreter** to format the file.
- Use **Split** to segregate concatenated columns and use **Pivot** to transform Rows to Columns.
- Data preparation may include renaming columns, creating hierarchies, Groups and calculations.

Q31. What are the best practices of data preparation in Tableau?
Ans.
Data should be prepared so that it improves user experience and helps in development of visualizations.

- The Data source should be given a user friendly name. Right click on Data Source and select **Rename**.
- Dimension and Measure columns should be given user friendly names. Right click on a field and select **Rename**.
- Check the data types of the fields. If data types are incorrect then change the datatypes in Tableau.
- Related fields should be organized in **Folders**. Right click on a field and select **Group By/ Folder**.
- Hierarchies help in drill downs. Identify the columns to be included **Hierarchy**. Create Hierarchy by Shift or Ctrl select the columns to be included in Hierarchy, right click and select Hierarchy.

- Provide **Aliases** to give meaningful description to the values. For example, if Region is SZ, you can alias it to South Zone.
- **Hide** the columns, dimensions and measures which are not used in the calculations or the view.
- Create Calculations to achieve required functionality. Name calculations in a user friendly manner.
- Apply appropriate filters to get meaning full data.
- Use extract when possible. Extracts are faster than live connection.
- Save the datasource as TDS file. This file can be shared and other developers can use this file for development.

Q32. On a chart, a user wants to drill down from Category to Sub- Category. What data transformation should be applied to achieve this functionality?
Ans.
In the Dimension section, create a hierarchy for Category and Sub-Category.

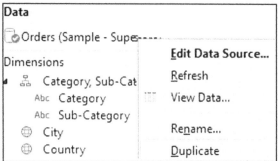

Exercise:
Use Tableau sample data source **Sample- Superstore.xls** located under \My Tableau Repository\Data sources.
Use **Orders** data sheet and prepare data for dash boarding.
Refer to downloaded workbook – Review Dimensions and Measures.

Q33. How to create a copy of the data source? In what scenarios it will be useful?

Ans.

Copy of a data source can be made by right clicking on it and selecting **Duplicate**.

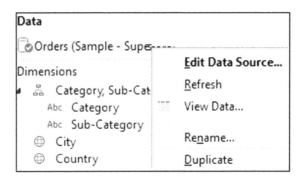

Copy of the data source can be useful when you have to create additional view/s of the same data source to create some visualizations like two separate charts for Year by Year comparisons.

Q34. In a multi-developer environment, how do we make sure that all the developers are using the same datasource structure?

Ans.

To ensure that all the developers are using the same data source, right click on the datasource and **Publish on the Tableau Server**.

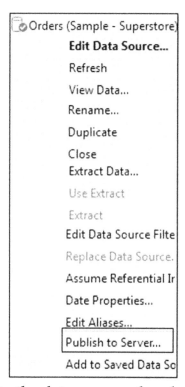

While connecting to the datasource, other developers can connect to the datasource from the Tableau server option.

Developers using the published datasource will be allowed to create their own calculations on the data source.

Q35. What is a TDE file and how it is created?
Ans.
Tableau Data Extract (TDE) file is a data extract or snap shot of the data. TDE files can be created by right clicking on the data source and selecting **Extract Data.**

- When an extract is created, the symbol of the datasource icon changes to two cylinders.

- Extracts result in better performance as compared to live connection.
- Extracts are useful in offline access of data. Extracts can be saved locally and do not require live connection to the source data.
- Extract is a snapshot of data, it needs to be **refreshed** as underlying data changes.
- Filters can be applied while creating an extract.
- While creating an extract data can be aggregated by dimensions.
- Extract can be created for all the rows or incrementally.
- Extract refreshes can be scheduled to run.

Exercise:
Use Tableau sample data source **Sample- Superstore.xls** located under \My Tableau Repository\Data sources
Use **Orders** datasheet to create a TDE file. Review the file after the data extract and see changes in the datasource icon.

Q36. What is a .TDS file?
Ans. A TDS file stores the data source connection information. Developers can connect to the TDS file to get the data source details. TDS file is created by right clicking on the data source and selecting "Add to Saved Data Sources"

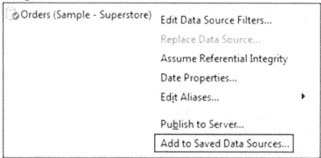

TDS file is in XML format and contains the following information
- Data Source Type.
- Data Source connection details such as Server, Port, Location of local files.
- Joins, tables joined and type of join.
- Groups
- Sets
- Calculated fields
- Bins
- Default field properties such as number formats, aggregation and sort Order.

Exercise:
Use the file you have created in the previous section and save the data source as .TDS file under \My Tableau Repository\Data sources.

Navigate to the above path and open .Tds file and review it in a notepad.

Q37. Developer needs to create a chart where data is coming from 2 different sources. How you can combine data from these two data sources and display it in the chart?
Ans.
Data Blending is used when there are 2 independent data sources and visualization needs to merge the data from these data sources.

- In Data blending, one datasource becomes primary and the second data source becomes secondary.
- Data blending is not a join. Join occurs between the tables from the same data source.
- To perform data blending there should be at least one common column between the data sources.
- If a common field does not exist, then edit the relationship between the datasources. To edit relationship, navigate to **menu** and select **Data/Edit Relationships**.
- Data blending can be applied per visualization, it is does not carry over to the entire workbook.

Q38. How are primary and secondary datasources identified in data blending?
Ans.
Primary data source has a blue check mark and secondary has an orange check mark.

Q39. You have to show data in a chart. This data is stored in 2 tables in Oracle database called "Sales Structure". What technique should be used - data blending or joins?
Ans.
A Join will be more appropriate in this scenario because data source is same.

Q40. What is data aggregation?
Ans. Tableau aggregates data automatically when measure is placed on the view canvas. Default aggregation is **Sum**. But it can be changed to any other type of aggregation.

Q41. A Source data table has 100,000 rows of data. Every month around 10,000 new rows get added to this table. What option you will choose to load only the new rows?
Ans.
This can be accomplished by creating an extract and choosing incremental load option.

Q42. Filters can be created from Dimension and Measures. To which SQL keyword do they correspond?
Ans.
Dimension filters are similar to **WHERE** clause in SQL query. Measure filter is similar to the **HAVING** clause.

Q43. How does Pills work in Tableau?
Ans.
When a field is placed from the data window into the view canvas, Tableau creates a **pill**. Whether a pill is dimension or measure or continuous or discreet affects the analysis and the view.

- Pill can contain continuous or discreet data. **Continuous** data can take any value in a range. **Discreet** data have distinct separate values.
- **Dimensions** are discreet and **Measures** are continuous.
- Discreet pills are **blue** in color and continuous are **green** in color.
- Dimension and Measure can be changed to discreet or continuous by right clicking and selecting the desired type.
- When a **continuous** pill is dropped into the view it creates an **axis**.
- When a **discreet** pill is dropped into the view, it creates a **label/header**.
- **Color** is also decided depending on whether - the pill is continuous or discreet.
- Filtering on a discreet field such as category will ask for the specific values.

- Filtering the continuous field such as profit, will first ask if you want to filter at the row level or
- Aggregate level and then brings up options for continuous ranges.

Q44. How is color created in a Map?
Ans.

- In Maps, the default color depends on whether a field is continuous or discreet.
- A measure on **Color** will create a **filled** map. A dimension on the color will create a **Symbol** map. But whether color is gradient or palette still depends on whether the pill/field is continuous or discreet.

Exercise:
Use Tableau sample data source **Sample- Superstore.xls** located under \My Tableau Repository\Data sources.
Create a Map by using State and Region in one sheet and State and Sales in another sheet.
Refer to downloaded workbook – sheet/s - SymbolMap_Color and FilledMap_Color.

Q45. How to organize/structure your workbook?
Ans.
It is important to structure your workbook for ease of use and development.

- Fields can be organized in folders. Keep related fields in a folder.
- Hide all unused fields.
- Workbook many contain multiple sheets and dashboards. Color related sheets and dashboards.
- Hide unused worksheets.

Q46. How to change/replace the data source after developing visualizations or dashboard?

Ans.

Datasource can be replaced by following the below steps:

- Add new datasource to Tableau. Navigate to main menu and select Data/New Data Source

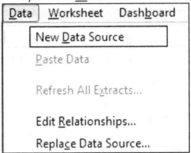

- Make sure the new data source contains the same data structure in terms of calculations, hierarchies, parameters etc.
- Right click on the old datasource and select **Replace data.**

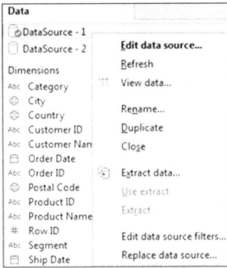

- Select the Current and Replacement datasources

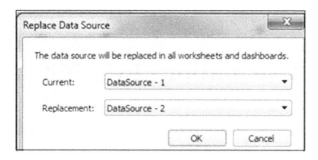

- After replacing the datasource, close the original datasource.

Q47. Which fields get automatically generated in Tableau?
Ans.
Tableau generates few fields automatically in the data window. These fields get generated when you connect to the data and create a sheet. These fields are **Measure Names**, **Measure Values** and **Number of Records**.

Q48. What is Data interpreter?
Ans.
Sometimes the source data is not in the right format. Headers and rows are not stored correctly in the excel file. In such scenarios, Tableau invokes "Data interpreter".
Data interpreter option is invoked automatically when Tableau recognizes that data is not in the right format.

Data Interpreter formats the data correctly and also provides you option to Pivot the columns into rows.

3
Calculations in Tableau

Q49. What are the different types of Calculations available in Tableau?

Ans.

Calculations or calculated field/s help in enhancing your visualization and implementing business rules. Calculated fields are created by using different Tableau functions.

Types of calculations available are:

- **Regular Calculation**. This calculation is sent to the data source for processing and the result is returned to Tableau.
- **Table Calculation**. Calculation occurs on top of the returned result set or chart.
- **Quick Table Calculation**. These calculations are predefined Table calculations provided by Tableau.
- **Level of Detail (LOD) calculation**. This calculation computes aggregation that is out of the level of detail of the view.

Q50. How to create a Regular calculation?

Ans.

Regular calculation can be created by right clicking on the white space in the data section and selecting "Create Calculated Field".

Calculated field can also be created by navigating to the Menu/Analysis and selecting **Create Calculated Field**.

Calculated field can use any of the Tableau defined functions such as

Exercise:
Use Tableau sample data source **Sample- Superstore.xls** located under \My Tableau Repository\Data sources.
Use Orders Data sheet. Create a calculation for Sales with Discount. **Use the formula** :

                    Sales * Discount.
Refer to downloaded workbook – Sheet - Regular Calculation.

Q51. How is Table calculation created?

Ans.

Since Table calculation works on the returned result set or the chart, it can be created on the view canvas.

Create a visualization by placing dimension and measures on the view canvas.

Click on the measure pill and select **Add Table Calculation**.

Table calculation can also be created just like regular calculation but will use the **Table calculation functions.**

Exercise:

Use Tableau sample data source **Sample- Superstore.xls** located under \My Tableau Repository\Data sources.
Use Orders data sheet. Place State on **Rows** and Sales on the **Columns** Shelf. Click on the Pill to add Table Calculation for **Rank**
Refer the downloaded workbook- sheet - Table Calculation_Rank.

Q52. What are Quick Table calculations in Tableau?
Ans.
Tableau provides some pre-defined Table calculations called Quick Table calculations.
Quick Table calculations also works on returned result set and is created by right clicking on the measure pill on the view canvas and selecting "Quick Table Calculation"
The types of quick calculations available are

Running Total

Difference

Percent Difference

Percent of Total

Rank

Percentile

Moving Average

YTD Total

Compound Growth Rate

Year over Year Growth

YTD Growth

Q53. What is Addressing and Partitioning of Data?
Ans.
Tableau internally assigns all fields in the dataset to be addressing or partitioning.

Partitioning field partitions data into separate individual sections. Calculations are applied to these sections.
Addressing field provides the direction in which the calculation will take place.

Exercise:
Use Tableau sample data source **Sample- Superstore.xls** located under \My Tableau Repository\Data sources.
Use the **Orders** data sheet.
Place Order Date on the **Rows**, drill down to Quarters. Double click on Sales. Create a Table calculation for "Running Total". After the visualization is created, navigate to Sum(Sales) and select **edit Table calculation**.
Under **Running Along**, choose the option for **Advanced** and see which columns are used for Partitioning and Addressing. Switch the columns around to see the changes in the output.

Refer the downloaded workbook- sheet - AddressingPartioning.

Q54. What is First (), Last () and Index () functions in Tableau?
Ans.
Refer to Partitioning field's definition in the previous question.
First, Last and Index Table calculation functions provide information about the position of a data element within a partition.

First() – returns the number of rows from the current row to the first row in the partition. It is a negative number.

Last () – returns the number of rows from the current row to the last row in the partition. It is a positive number.

Index() – returns the index of the current row in the partition. The first row index starts with 1.

Exercise:
Create an example to understand First, Last and Index functions.
Place **Category** on the **Rows** and drill down to **Sub-Category**. Place Sales on the Columns. Create calculations for First(),Last() and Index() and place them on the Table in the view canvas. Observe the output.
Navigate to the function pills on the left under **Marks** and use **Compute using** to change the partitioning fields and see the difference in your output.

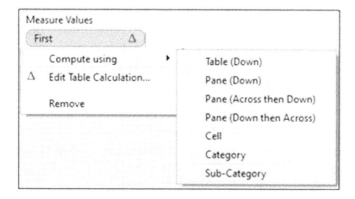

Refer the downloaded workbook- sheet - IndexFirstLast.

Q55. What are LOD (Level of Detail) calculations in Tableau?
Ans.
LOD calculations compute aggregation that is outside the "level of detail" of the view.
LOD expression has a specific syntax and works with keywords such as Include, Exclude and Fixed. LOD calculation follows the below syntax

{Keyword [Dim1],[Dim2]: Sum(Measure field)}

Q56. Explain keywords in LOD expressions?
Ans.
LOD expressions have the following keywords

- **Fixed** computes the value using the mentioned dimensions ignoring the dimension in the view
- **Include** computes the value using the mentioned dimension in addition to the dimensions in the view
- **Exclude** will ignore the mentioned dimension. It ignores the dimension even if it is used in the view.
- If no dimension or Keyword is specified then the expression is "Table scoped" which is the complete aggregate of the data. {Sum(Sales)}
- Only field names can be used in Dimension declaration. Calculated fields can be used but not the calculation expression. Sets, parameters or Table calculations are not allowed.
- The LOD expressions that use Exclude or Include always result in measure. These results cannot be binned.

- Fixed can be an expression or a dimension based on the aggregation used. If the aggregate expression results in measure then the overall expression will be a measure. If aggregation such as string, Boolean or Date types results in dimension then the overall expression will be a dimension. Fixed expression can be converted to a dimension or a measure.
- Numeric Fixed LOD expressions can be binned unless the aggregate expression is a date.

Q57. Visualization displays Sum (Profit) by Zipcode. In the same visualization, the user also wants to see "Sum (Profit) at the State level". What kind of function should be used in such scenario?

Ans.

LOD expressions are used to aggregate outside the level of detail of the view. In this case the level of detail is defined by ZipCode. So if a developer wants to calculate the Sum by Profit at the State level, he can create a calculated field with the following LOD expression and place this calculated field in the **Detail** shelf.

$$\{Fixed\ [State]: SUM\ ([Profit])\}$$

This expression will compute at the State level. It will ignore the dimension in the view i.e. ZipCode.

Refer the downloaded workbook- sheet - LOD_Fixed.

Q58. What is Attr function?

Ans.

Attr checks to see if there is only one value for a given field for all rows in a result set. Attr is used to aggregate the dimension. Whenever we need to check for a single value such as if State = "NJ", use Attr

Q59. When using Dimension field with a measure field in a calculation, you get the following error. What is the resolution of the error?

Ans.

This error occurs when a dimension is used with aggregated function. If the dimension returns more than one row of data, this error occurs. This error can be resolved by using **ATTR** function with the dimension.

Q60. Source data contains the EmpID and Name in the format **EmpID-Name**. How will you separate the EmpID and Name into 2 fields?
Ans.
On the data window, navigate to the field.
Right click on the field, select **Transform** and **Split**.
Split will split the columns using the delimiter **-.** The split function will create two separate columns- EmpID and Name.

Q61. How are dates handled in Tableau?
Ans.
Tableau provides different options and functions to manage dates effectively.
- Date property can be set by right clicking on the data source in the Data section and select Date properties. **Week Start** day can be selected. Also there is an option to specify a **Fiscal Year Start** Month. The Developer can also specify the **Date Format** to be followed in the design.

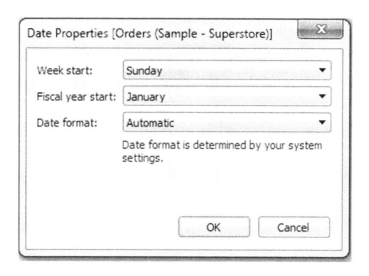

- Dates can be **Discreet** or **Continuous**. Date level of a field can be changed by dropping it into the Row or Column shelf and selecting pill drop menu. Using this menu, dates can be changed between discreet and continuous.

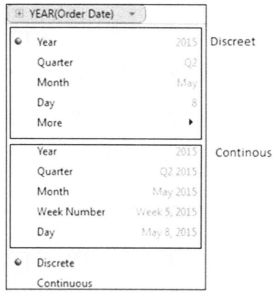

- Sometimes Dates are not interpreted correctly by Tableau and dates - comes as String or some other format. In such cases, a field can be converted to Date in Tableau. On the data window, right click on the field and select "Change Data Type".
- Custom date format can be created by right clicking on the date field and selecting **Create Custom Date**.
- Dates functions available in Tableau are

Q62. A Developers need to calculate the difference between two dates – Order Date and Ship Date. Which function will be best suited?

Ans.

DATEDIFF('day',[Order Date],[Ship Date])

4
Visualizations

Q63. What is a visualization?
Ans.
Visualization is a pictorial representation of data.

Q64. How is visualization created in Tableau?
Ans.
In Tableau visualization is created on a **Sheet**.

- To create any visualization, the developer needs to drop **Dimension** and/or **Measure** on the view canvas.
- When you drop a measure in the view canvas, Tableau automatically **aggregates** the data. Default aggregation is **Sum**. These aggregations can be changed to other types.
- **Show Me** feature suggests the best visualization for the number of Dimensions and Measures selected.
- Dimensions or measures can be used to create filters and quick filters. These filters or quick filters help in providing context to the data.
- Visualization can have **Color**, **calculated field**, **Shape** and **Size**.
- One or multiple Sheets are combined to create **Dashboard**.
- Sheets and Dashboards are used to create a **Story**.

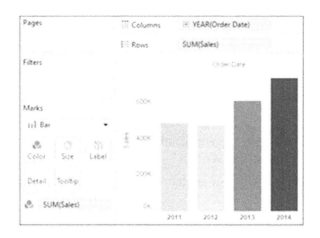

Q65. How are Maps created in Tableau?

Ans.

- Maps are created for the geographical or location fields.
- Tableau automatically identifies geographical fields like County, State, City and zip-codes. It assigns Latitude and Longitude to each value of the field based on the data present in Tableau Map Server.
- Fields having the geographical role assigned, can be identified by a **globe** symbol next to them.
- Sometimes Tableau cannot recognize a field as a geographical location. For example, sometimes Zip code would be identified as number. In such instances you can right click and assign a geographical role to the field.
- If Tableau does not contain the desired Latitudes and Longitudes, you can define them in a database or a csv file.

  Geographical roles available in Tableau are

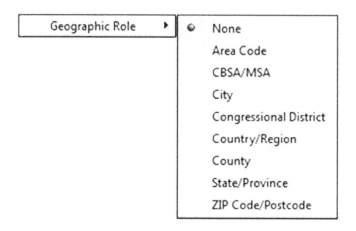

- o Area code contains USA telephone area codes.
- o CBSA/MSA denotes USA metropolitan Statistical Areas.
- o City represents worldwide cities with population more than 15,000.
- o Congressional District represents U.S. congressional districts.
- o County/Region represents worldwide countries.
- o County represents counties of few countries such a USA, France, German etc.
- o State/Province represents worldwide states.
- o Zip code/ Postalcode of selected countries are available

Exercise:

Use Tableau sample data source **Sample- Superstore.xls** located under \My Tableau Repository\Data sources.

Use **Orders** data sheet. Place **State** on Rows and **Sales** on the Column Shelf. This will create a Map which will give Sales for each State.

Refer the downloaded workbook- sheet - FilledMap_Color.

Q66. When a developer uses City and Sales to generate a Map, "146 unknown" is displayed at the bottom of the Map. How can this issue be resolved?
Ans.
"146 Unknown" means Tableau is unable to plot some 146 cities. Some of the cities may also be duplicate.
In such a scenario, drop State on the **Detail** shelf.
Alternatively, you can click on "146 Unknown" and from the popup dialogue box select "Edit Locations"

Q67. How is data granularity maintained in Tableau?
Ans.
In Tableau, granularity of data is defined by the **Dimensions** field.
Dimension field dropped in **Detail** shelf will change the granularity of the visualization.
Dropping measure in the **Detail** shelf will have no effect.

Q68. What is ToolTip and how to provide a Tool Tip?
Ans.
Tooltip is a shelf next to **Detail**.
- Tooltip displays the data description, when the user hovers over the data elements of the chart.

- Tooltip displays the data elements that are in the view canvas. You can display other data elements by placing them on the **Detail**. Use those data elements that do not change the granularity of the data.
- Tool Tip can be formatted to add different colors and fonts.
- Any comments can also be displayed in the ToolTip.
  The screen shot given below shows Tooltip when the user hovers over a state in the Map.

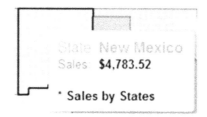

Q69. How to make sure that all the sheets have the same look and feel?

Ans.

Complete all the formatting changes on one sheet, say, Source Sheet. Right click on the sheet and select **Copy Formatting**.

Go to the Target Sheet or other sheets - where you want to copy the formatting, right click on the sheet and select "**Paste formatting**".

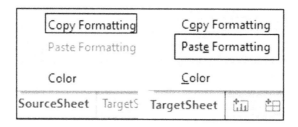

Q70. Source data contains several Sub-categories - Binders, Bookcases, Chairs and Copiers. The requirement is to combine all these Sub-categories into a new dimension called "Office Supplies". What technique can be used to achieve this requirement?

Ans.

Fields can be combined into a new dimension by creating a **Group**.

Groups are used to combine different dimension values. Once grouped, these values show up as a new dimension field under **Dimensions.** Group is also used to improve data quality in a dashboard. For eg., if visualization contains values such as Unites States, USA, US , you can combine all these values into one Group and have a value like USA.

Q71. How is a Group created?

Ans.

A Group can be created from the view canvas such as from Table, Bar chart or Scatter chart.

On a Bar chart, select the headers of a dimension and click on the "pin" icon.

On a scatter chart, highlight the marks on the chart and click on the "pin" icon to group.

Group can also be created in the data window. Group can also be calculated by creating calculated field.

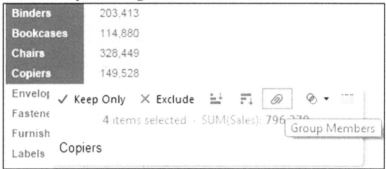

Exercise:

Use Tableau sample data source **Sample- Superstore.xls**
Use Orders data sheet. Create a Group called Office Supplier –
Group.
Refer the downloaded workbook- sheet - Group.

Q72. What are Bins in Tableau?
Ans.

Bins are used to convert a continuous measure or dimension into
discreet buckets. Bins, when created, display as a field under
Dimensions.

Bins are created by right clicking on a measure field and
selecting Create/Bins. Tableau suggests a size of the Bin or it
can be entered by the developer.

Bins can also be created by using a calculated field.

Q73. How do colors work in Tableau?
Ans.

In Tableau, measures or dimensions are colored by placing
them on the **Color** Shelf.

- Color of a data element is decided by it being continuous
  or discreet.
- A discreet field on the Color shelf, produces a "color
  palette". A continuous field creates a "gradient".

- Click on the color shelf to **Edit Colors**. To display consistent color, double click on the color and provide HTML code or RGB values.

Q74. How to create custom color palette in Tableau?
Ans.
Custom color palette can be provided to Tableau by modifying the **Prefrences.tps** file. It is an XML file and is located under "My Tableau Repository" folder on your machine or where Tableau desktop is installed.
If no custom color is specified, this file appears with place holder such as

<?xml version='1.0'?>

Custom color can be specified in this file by using the HTML tags for Color Type and hexadecimal value.

Q75. Developer wants to create a "subset of data" such as "Top 10 customers by sales". This subset of data can be used as a filter in other sheets. What visualization technique should be used in such a scenario?
Ans.
Sets are used to create sub-set of the data based on a condition such as, Top 10 Customers by sales.
- Sets can be created manually from the visualization in view canvas. On a scatter graph, highlight the marks which you want to use to create a Set, and select **Create Set** by clicking on the **overlapping circle** icon from the popup tool bar.
- Sets can also be created dynamically from the data section. Right click on any dimension and select Create/Sets. On the dialogue box, navigate to **Top**

- Sets can be used with other sets. Sets can be used as a filter. They can also be used in a calculated field.
- Sets once created, show up in the data section below Measures.
- Sets are available in all the sheets and can be used in multiple visualizations.

Exercise:
Use Tableau sample data source **Sample- Superstore.xls**
Use Orders data sheet. Create a SET for Top 10 Customers by Sales.
Refer the downloaded workbook- sheet - Sets.

Q76. What is the difference between Sets and Filters?
Ans.
Sets and filters are similar with few differences.

- A set can be used as a filter. Filters are available only in one sheet but Sets are available as a part of data and therefore available in any sheet you create.
- Since Set becomes a part of the data, it is available when the datasource is saved as a .TDS file and shared across other dashboards.
- Sets get created automatically when **Action** is used in a dashboard.
- Sets get created, when **User filter** is applied to the dashboard for security.

Q77. What are the best practices of developing visualization in Tableau?

Ans.

Best practices should be followed to keep the design clean. Data should be organized and visualization should be easy to understand.

- Use folders to organize related fields or calculations.
- Name the data connections appropriately.
- Use standard naming conventions for the calculated fields.
- Use standard naming convention for the parameters.
- Use standard naming conventions to name the sheets and dashboards.

Q78. What are the charts types available in Tableau?

Ans.

Tableau provides different kinds of visualization objects. **Show Me** option shows all the charts available. Based on selected dimensions and measures, Tableau shows the suggested charts in "Show Me"

Q79. What are the data elements required to create a chart?
Ans.
Most of the charts require one or more dimensions and one or more Measures/expressions.

Q80. What chart should be used to show the relationship between two measures, say Sales and Quantity?
Ans.
The relationship between two measures is displayed using a Scatter chart.

Q81. A user wants to see - Sales and Profit by Region on the same chart. Sales should be displayed as a bar and Profit as a Line. What kind of visualization should be created?
Ans.
Combo chart or combination chart should be used to display 2 measures by a dimension.
Place Region on the **Columns** Shelf. Drop Sales and Profit on the Rows shelf.
Right click on the pill of Profit and select **Dual axis**.
Click on Sum(Sales) pill and change the **Mark Type** to **Bar**
Click on Sum(Profit) pill and change the **Mark Type** to Line.

Exercise:
Use the **Orders** data sheet.
Create the above combo chart for Sales and Profit by Region.
Refer the downloaded workbook- sheet - Combo Chart.

Q82. What are Filters? How many types of Filters are there in Tableau?
Ans.
Filters help in restricting or excluding data. Filters are applied independent of each other. Each time a filter is applied a separate query is sent to the data source. Exceptions to the rule are the "Context filters".

Tableau provides different types of filters.

- Data Source filters. These filters are added to the data source. These filters restrict whole data.

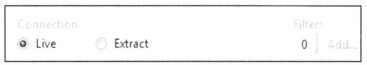

- Extract filters. These filters are implemented while creating an extract. Right click on the datasource and select **Extract data**. In the extract data options, select the filter/s.

- Context filters. These filters create a subset of data. Context filter, if applied, acts like a temp table. All the other filters act on this sub-set of data.
- Quick filters. These filters give the user an option to select a filter while viewing a dashboard or a visualization. Place a field on the **Filters** shelf, right click and select "Show filter"

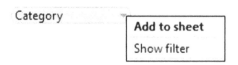

Q83. What is the difference between using Dimension as a filter and Measure as a filter?
Ans.
Usually Dimensions are discreet and Measures are continuous. When a Dimension field is used as a filter, it displays as separate categories in a List or a Drop-down.
If Measure field is used as a filter, it gets displayed as a slider.

Q84. What is a parameter?
Ans.
- Parameters provide a dynamic value to the hardcoded or constant value in a visualization.
- Parameters are single select and provide context only when used in a calculated field.
- Parameters can work as a data input to the visualization.
- A good use of parameter will be, for example, if you want to change the measure in a chart based on the values selected by a user.
- Parameters are displayed at the bottom of the data section.

Q85. Is Parameter a filter?
Ans.
Parameter is not a filter but can work with a filter.

Q86. There are 3 measures – Sales, Profit and Quantity. A Developer wants change the visualization based on user selection of these measures. What technique should be used to achieve this requirement?
Ans.
This can be done by creating a string parameter, say "Param select Measure" for these measures.
Use this parameter in a calculated field, say, "Select Measure"
Create a visualization using this calculated field Select Measure.

Display the "Param Select Measure" for user selection.

Exercise:
Create a new sheet, use Region, Sales, Profit and Quantity. Create a parameter, so that user can pick a measure from the list and it should change the measure in the visualization. *Refer the downloaded workbook- sheet - Parameters.*

Q87. In how many ways can Sorting be done in Tableau?
Ans.
Sorting means arranging data in ascending, descending or customized order.

- Sorting can be ascending or descending. Sorting can be on dimensions or measures.
- Sorting option can be selected from the tool bar.

  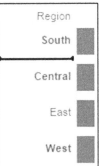

- Sorting option is also available when you mouse hover over the axis of a chart.
- Pill sorting option is available only for dimensions.
- Sorting can also be performed by dragging and dropping data elements on a chart.

  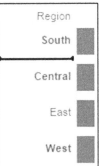

- Color legends also can be sorted by manually.

5

Dashboards and Visual Story

Q88. What is a Dashboard?

Ans.

BI dashboards are similar to the car dashboard.

Car dashboard provides the complete status of the working of a car, such as, Gas, mileage, Air pressure and so on.

BI Dashboard provides a snapshot of the organization or Key Performance Indicator (KPI).

Q89. How are Dashboards are in Tableau?

Ans.

Dashboards in Tableau are created by either clicking on the

Dashboard icon at the bottom of the screen or from the Menu/ Dashboard.

- Dashboards contain one or multiple sheets.
- **Actions** provide interactivity to the dashboards.
- Filters present in the individual sheets are to dashboards too. These filters can be applied to a specific sheet or all sheets using the datasource.
- Dashboard contains "Dashboard Objects". These objects are available in the left pane. These dashboard objects are layout containers – horizontal or vertical. These objects can be used to add Image, webpage, text and Blank container. Use these objects to enhance your dashboard.
- Dashboard size and sheet coordinates can also be specified.

Exercise:
Create Dashboard using Sheets, FilledMap_color, Combo chart, Parameters and TableCalculation_Rank.
Refer the downloaded workbook- sheet - Db_SalesDashboard.

Q90. How can interactivity be achieved in a dashboard?
Ans.
Interactivity between dashboards is achieved by the use of "Actions".

Q91. What are Actions?
Ans.
Actions provide interactivity to the dashboards.
Actions can be of different types
- Filter Actions. This type of Action is used to create interaction between the sheets in a dashboard.
- Highlight Actions. It is used to color the selected Marks on a chart.

- URL Actions. This type of Action is used to create a hyperlink to another webpage.
- Actions can be configured by navigating to Menu – Dashboard/Actions.

Q92. A developer has created a dashboard using 4 sheets, say, FilledMap_color, Combo chart, Parameters and TableCalculation_Rank. How can he make sure that when the user clicks on a data element on one chart, the other charts are also filtered with that data element?
Ans.
"Use as filter" property in a chart, makes the data element in that chart act as a filter to other sheets/charts.
On the desired chart, click on the pull down menu on the right and select **Use as Filter**.

Q93. What is Story in Tableau?
Ans.
Story uses dashboards and sheets to provide detail information about a measure or KPI.
Sheets or Dashboards make up a **Story**. A Story can contain multiple tabs. Story is created like any other sheet by clicking

on the icon at the bottom of the screen

Exercise:
If you have created different sheets and dashboards using the previous exercises, create a **Story** by using FilledMap_Color,Db_SalesDashboard and Sets sheets/Dashboards.
Refer the downloaded workbook- sheet - Sales Story

Q94. How will you deploy Tableau workbook on the server?
Ans.
Tableau workbook can be published to the Tableau Server by using Tableau Desktop.
 • Open your workbook on Tableau desktop.
 • Navigate to Menu/Server and select **Publish Workbook**

 • It will ask you for the server credentials. On successful login, you will get the options to publish your entire workbook or specific sheets.
 • Entire workbook or specific sheets in a workbook can be published.

Q95. In a visualization, you have data for all the Segments. In the source data, Users are assigned to a specific Segments. Requirement is that the users should see data only for their assigned Segments. What technique should be used to achieve this requirement?

Ans.

The above requirement can be fulfilled by creating **User Filter** in Tableau Desktop during design.

User Filter will work when Users login to the Tableau Server.

To implement User Filter, you should have to access to Tableau Server.

To create User filter, on Tableau Desktop, navigate to Menu-Server. Login to the Server.

Navigate to Menu – Server – Create User Filter using the Segment.

In this way when the User login's he will see the data only for his segment

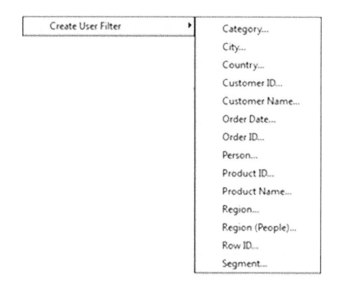

Q96. How will you schedule an data extract in Tableau?
Ans.

- Create an extract on Tableau desktop and configure it for Full refresh or incremental load.
- Navigate to your sheet and right click on your data source and select "Publish to Server"
- On Publish Data Source to Tableau Server dialogue, you can set the schedule.

- This will publish and set the schedule on the Server.
- This schedule can be modified any time.

6

Commonly Asked Questions

Q97. Tableau can connect to different data sources but on my version of Tableau desktop, I see only limited data source options.
Ans.
You have installed Tableau desktop personal edition. Personal edition allows you to connect to only excel and text files. All the other data sources are available with the licensed version.

Q98. Multiple users in different departments are developing dashboards. How to make sure that dashboards will show a single version of the truth and the enterprise wide solution is delivered?
Ans.
We should implement some practices that will ensure the enterprise wide implementation

- Data source should be created only once. All the common transformations and calculations should be present in this data source.
- Data source should be shared with other users creating the dashboards. Data Source/s can be shared by publishing them on the server or by creating a TDS file.
- Look and feel of the dashboard should be the same. Color scheme, fonts etc. should be decided and implemented in all the dashboards.
- Create a dashboard review board that will review all the dashboards before moving to production. This will ensure that standards are maintained.

Q99. How does licensing work on Tableau server?
Ans.
Tableau Server licensing comes in two modes – User based or core based.

User based licensing restricts how many users can work on your installation of Tableau Server. Tableau Server can be installed on a single machine or multiple machines in a cluster.

Core-based licensing provides license on number of cores on a single machine installation or multi-node installation. It does not restrict the number of users in the system.

Q100. When a measure is placed on the view canvas - row or column, sometimes I see field prefixed by an aggregation function like **Sum** and at other times I see **Agg()**
Ans.
Tableau automatically aggregates measures on the view canvas. Default aggregation in Sum.

When you drop a measure field, the aggregation applied is **Sum**. This aggregation can be changed to Average or any other type.

When an "aggregated measure" is used in a calculation and then the calculation is placed on the view canvas, it shows **Agg** in front of the calculated column. It means that aggregation is built within the calculation. This aggregation cannot be changed.

Q101. How will you load new and updated rows of data in Tableau?
Ans.
Create an extract and choose the incremental load option.

Q102. How big should be the Tableau TDE file?
Ans.
Tableau Data Extract (TDE) file is an extract of data and it depends on the size of the source data. As it is a compressed file, it will be smaller than the original size of the source data.

Q103. I have created a TDS and TDSX file. Which file will be bigger and why?
Ans.
TDSX file will be a larger file as it is packaged with data.

Q104. What is What-if analysis and how is it implemented?
Ans.
What-if scenario involves accepting user input in the dashboard and changing the calculations based on the user input. A good example will be discount offered, where the user wants to know, at run time, how his overall profitability will change if he changes the discount price.
What-if analysis can be performed by the use of Parameters.

Q105. How to implement Tableau multi-developer environment?
Ans.
Multi-developer environment is required when a number of dashboards are to be developed by different developers.
In such an implementation/s, the team can be divided into data modelers and dashboard designers. Alternatively, one complete dashboard can be assigned to a single developer. But when the dashboard is huge then multiple developers can work on the same dashboard and create visualization in separate workbooks.
There can be many ways to implement such scenarios
- Data modeler/s create data sources and save it as TDS file or publish to the server. This will ensure that all data standards and transformations are maintained.

- Developers connect to this published data source to develop dashboards.
- If sheets are developed by different developers, then they can be merged into single dashboard by performing copy/paste.
- Once all sheets are merged into one workbook, there will be many data sources as data sources are tied to the sheets. These data sources are to be replaced by the primary data source and all other data sources can be closed.

Q106. Can I copy and paste the visualization from one Tableau workbook to another?
Ans.
You can copy a visualization or a sheet from one Tableau workbook to another. The Sheet is tied to the data source, so when you copy the sheet, to another workbook, the data source will be copied as well. You can always replace this new data source with the one in the copied workbook and close the datasource which is no longer in use.

Q107. Source table contains different data elements without any header information, what techniques should be applied to categorize all those fields and have common name for such data elements.
Ans.
On a scatter plot, highlight all such data elements and create a Group. This group will be displayed as a field in the Dimension section, which can be renamed.

Q108. How to test a Tableau application?
Ans.
A Tableau application should be tested at multiple levels. The basic principle is to always compare against the source data

- Check it against the original data source. Check the count of rows in Tableau by using "Number of Records" measure and source table.
- Compare the aggregations in the charts against the database SQL.
- For excel data sources, use excel filters and formulas.
- Export the data out of Tableau, by right clicking on the chart and selecting view data

Q109. What should be the size of a Tableau workbook?
Ans.
The size of the workbook depends on the specific requirement. There is no single size. Size of the dashboard depends on the data, number of objects and functionality of the dashboard.

Q110. How you will open a twb bigger than 4GB in size?
Ans.
If the dashboard size is larger than the RAM size of your computer then you can open it on the server which will have more RAM.

Q111. What is Performance Recording on Tableau desktop?
Ans.
- Performance recording feature records performance information on the various events on a dashboard as users interact with the worksheet and visualization.
- This feature can be turned-on on the Tableau desktop, and can be turned-off once the recording is done.
- This feature records performance information on the various events on a dashboard as users interact with the worksheets and visualization.

- It creates a workbook under \Documents\My Tableau Repository\Logs. The name of this workbook is similar to performance_20160808T084552_11184.tab.
- This workbook can be analyzed for performance metrics.
- To turn-on performance recording, navigate to help on the menu and select.

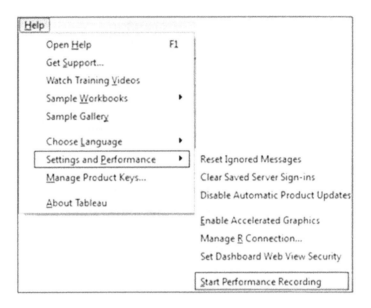

Q112. How to performance tune Tableau data model and dashboard?

Ans.

Some of the ways to improve performance of a Tableau dashboard

- Use **performance recorder** to gain knowledge of the performance of different sheets and actions in a workbook.
- Use extracts, if possible. Extracts are faster than live connection.
- Minimize the number of fields in your workbook. Hide fields which are not required.

- Reduce the number of filters used on a worksheet and dashboard. In Tableau, filters are applied separately and each time a query is sent to the data source. Multiple filters will slow down the application.
- All complex calculations should be performed at the data source level.
- Number of sheets will affect the performance. Delete or hide any unused sheets.

Q113. In your visualization, you want show - if the Sales is greater than 15000 then "Good Sales" else "Not so good sales". What kind of calculation you will use to implement this rule.

Ans.

This scenario can be implemented by creating a regular calculation. For example,

```
Sales-Good-Bad                          Sample - Superstore

If Sum([Sales]) > 150000 then "Good Sales"
else "Not so good"
end
```

Q114. Developer wants to display different colors in a bar chart based on the following condition.

- If Sales is > 50,000 then display bar in a green color
- If Sales is < 50,000 then display bar in a red color.

He uses the following calculation and places it on the **Color** shelf. Will he get the desired color?

If (Sum([Sales]) > 50000) then "Green"
ELSEIF (Sum([Sales]) < 50000) then "Red"
END

Ans.

No. Green and Red in above calculation does not mean color. It is just a calculated field/measure. After placing this calculation on the **Color** shelf, automatic color will be displayed. To change to specific colors, developer should navigate to **Color** shelf, click on **Edit Colors** and set the desired colors.

Q115. You want to uninstall and reinstall Tableau desktop on our machine. What is the easiest way to take a backup of your existing data sources, workbooks and other Tableau related files?
Ans.
When you install Tableau desktop, it creates My Tableau Repository folder in your documents folder. The easiest way to back-up your previous work is to rename the existing "My Tableau Repository" folder and then uninstall or re-install Tableau

Q116. A developer has created an initial dashboard using a fields from the source data. In the next data run, the name of one of the fields used in the dashboard changed and the dashboard shows error. How can this error be resolved.
Ans.
The developer can right click on the field and select **Replace references** and select the new field.

Q117. Your new team is struggling in understanding Tableau dashboard designed by an ex-employee. There is no documentation or knowledge available. How you will understand the previously built workbook.
Ans.
Follow the steps below to understand a previously built workbook

- Review the data sources. Edit the data source to see if any filter is used while extracting the data. Check to see if the connection is a live connection or an extract.
- Developer may have renamed the dimensions and measures. Right click on the dimensions and measures and select **Describe** to get information on the source columns.
- Fields prefixed with = are calculated fields. Right click and edit to understand their definition.
- A delta symbol $\triangle$ next to the measure pill in the view, shows that Table Calculation is implemented. Edit Table Calculation to understand the definition.
- At the bottom of the data window look for Parameters and Sets. You can edit and view the definitions of these elements.
- Right click on the status bar and select "Unhide" to display the hidden sheets.
- See the symbols of the data source to understand if they are extracts and if using data blending.
- Check the output of the dashboards to see different sheets. See what data elements, objects, sheets are displayed on the dashboard.
- Check for any aliases in the fields.
- Look for the **Actions** in the dashboard. On the Menu, click on the "Dashboard" and navigate to "Actions".
- Locate the log files under "My Repository folder".

Q118. What are the best practices to be followed while creating a dashboard?
Ans.
While creating a dashboard, care should be taken so that the dashboard is be clean and easy to understand. The following practices can be followed

- Design a dashboard for a specific Screen resolution. Discuss with your user community and decide on a screen resolution that will cater to all the users
- Design a Screen layout which makes the navigation on the screen natural and easy.
- Avoid using complex calculations in the dashboard. Move such calculations to the data source.
- Use muted colors. So that focus is in the dashboard not on the color.
- Create a template and include all the layout related attributes on this template. Use this template to develop dashboards.

Q119. Dashboard displays Quick filter, say, Category. By default all the filters show (All) option. How can you turn this option off?

Ans.
From the pull down menu of the quick filter, select Customize and uncheck "Show "All" Value.

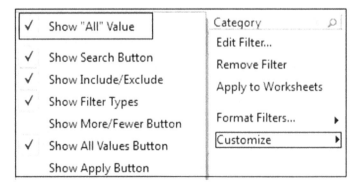

Q120. What development methodology is preferred in Tableau development – Agile or Waterfall?

Ans.

Tableau development should follow Agile methodology. Traditional methodology or water fall model, worked in a sequential order – Feasibility study, Requirements, Design, Testing, Deployment and support. This method though good for complex systems, considered to be time consuming in answering business questions at a rapid pace.

Agile methodology on other hand facilitated rapid development of application. Development team worked closely with the business users and helped in faster delivery of the application.

About The Author

AUTHOR NAME is Chandraish Sinha
Find out more at amazon.com/author/ChandraishSinha
Or visit www.LearnTableauPublic.com

Can I Ask A Favor?

If you enjoyed this book, found it useful or otherwise then I'd really appreciate it if you would post a short review on Amazon. I do read all the reviews personally so that I can continually write what people are wanting.

Thanks for your support!